TALPA
The Story of a Mole

COLLINS ANIMAL LIVES
Other books in this series

TALPA
The Story of a Mole

KENNETH MELLANBY

Illustrated by Bert Kitchen

COLLINS
ST JAMES'S PLACE · LONDON

William Collins Sons & Co Ltd
London · Glasgow · Sydney · Auckland
Toronto · Johannesburg

First published in Great Britain 1976
First published in paperback 1979
© text K. Mellanby 1976
© illustrations William Collins Sons & Co Ltd 1976
ISBN 0 00 195851 8
Printed in Great Britain by
William Collins Sons & Co Ltd, Glasgow

Contents

Foreword

The story of *Talpa* is the story of the first year in the life of a mole. It is about an individual, and I have given him a name in order to distinguish him from other moles in the story. I have chosen "Talpa" because it means "mole" in Latin.

Talpa's story has been made up from the stories of many real moles who have lived a normal life in the countryside of East Anglia, which is the area I know best. All the things that happen to Talpa happen to wild moles. Of course a single animal may not have all the different experiences described in this book, but it will spend most of its time in the same way that Talpa spends most of his time. Moles are solitary, and live nearly all of their lives by themselves. Young moles are driven out of their mother's burrow, they travel and eventually (if they are not eaten by a hawk, a heron or an owl) they settle down in a burrow of their own. They obtain most of their food when worms and insects fall into their burrows, not by digging for them. And, like all wild creatures, moles usually die by being eaten by one of their predators.

Sometimes I attribute feelings to Talpa and say that he is hungry, happy or frightened. Although we do not know exactly how a mole's mind works, I think it is reasonable to say that an animal is "hungry" when it seeks strenuously for food, that it is "happy" when warm and well fed, and that it is "frightened" when it runs away from an enemy.

I

Talpa's First Days

Talpa was just ten days old. He and his brother and two sisters had been born on April the tenth in their warm, dry nest made of hay and dead leaves under the ground in the big oak wood near to the fen. The nest was like a hollow football and filled an underground cavern. It was pitch dark, snug and warm, particularly when Talpa's mother came and nestled down with her babies.

Talpa was now nearly two inches long and he had started to grow a thin covering of soft fur. He was just beginning to take an interest in the world around him, though he could not yet crawl far enough to get out of the nest. Most of the time he lay still, sleeping, keeping close to his brother and sisters when his mother was away searching for food. He liked it when she came back, for then she made the babies warm and comfortable and gave them a meal of rich, creamy milk. So far Talpa had done little else but eat, sleep and grow. When he was born he was a tiny naked little thing, less than an inch long. Now he was beginning to look more like a mole.

The nest, in its cavern, had two openings which led into the underground burrows which were the mother mole's territory. It was in these burrows that she spent all her time when not nursing and sleeping with her babies. The tunnels were about three inches across, just wide enough so that she could run along without brushing the walls. The system of burrows was about a foot under the surface of the ground, and stretched for ten to fifteen yards in all directions, zigzagging and branching and covering quite a big area of ground. There was almost no trace of the burrows to be seen among the dog's mercury and bluebells, still in bud, which covered the ground in the oak wood.

In the burrow it was dark, except in one or two places where a crack in the soil allowed a chink of light to penetrate. But mother mole behaved just as if she could see in the dark. She ran along the narrow zigzagging tunnel very quickly and never banged into the walls. She

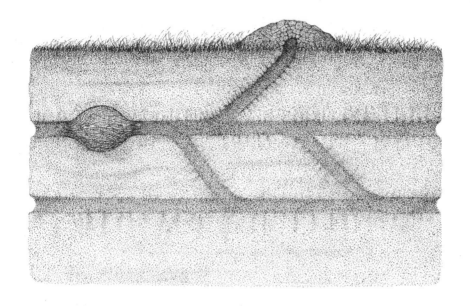

could find her food – worms and other animals –
without any difficulty. Moles have very tiny
eyes, and they cannot see in the daylight in the
way we do. They really "see" with their noses.
A mole has a snout something like a pig's,
smooth and pink with no fur on it. This snout
is very, very sensitive. It is able to detect the
faintest vibration in the air. When the mole is
running in its burrow, it makes vibrations which
hit the walls and are reflected back. We see
things with our eyes because light (which is
another kind of vibration) is reflected from
everything we see – even from the print of the
book we are reading. When we shut our eyes,

or go into a dark room, we cannot find our way about. But a blind person can learn to cope without sight, partly by sensing the vibrations in the air, in the same way as a mole – although the mole is better at doing this than any human being. The mole also uses its keen sense of smell to find food, and it can hear noises made by other animals. All these senses work together to tell the mole what is happening in the world around it. But it is its wonderful, super-sensitive nose that tells the mole most about its surroundings.

Today Talpa's mother woke up at eight o'clock in the morning. First she made sure that her four babies were safe and comfortable in the nest. She smoothed the hay and pushed a particularly knobbly oak leaf out of the way, and she gave the little moles their breakfast of milk and waited until they all fell asleep. Then she set off into the burrow, to find some food for herself. She ran very quietly so as not to disturb her prey. Soon she smelt a large, juicy earthworm which was crawling out of a hole in the wall. She seized the worm with her teeth, just in time to stop it from pulling back into the soil and disappearing. Then she got hold of the worm with her front paws. Moles' paws are big and flat, very good for digging in the earth, but they can also grasp large pieces of food.

Mother mole liked to start eating a worm by biting off its head, so she ran it through her paws, rather as if she were climbing up a rope. When she got to the front end of the worm, she gobbled it up quickly, her teeth making crackling noises on the tough skin. Then she wiped her mouth clean with the backs of her paws, and set off again down the tunnel.

Before long she smelt a small beetle, scurrying along in front of her. She made a snap at it with her teeth, but this time she missed and the beetle escaped into a crack in the soil. Mother mole did not worry, for she had already had a large worm and so was no longer ravenously hungry. But she had to eat a lot of food to make all the milk that her babies needed to grow.

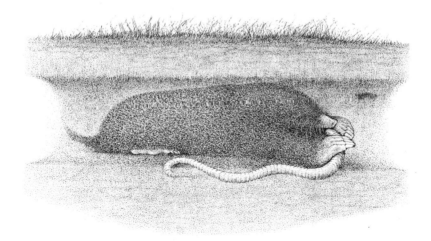

For the next two hours, mother mole ran up and down her burrows. She did not dig at all, but simply explored the whole network of tunnels looking for worms and insects which had fallen or burrowed into it. She found and ate another worm, not so big and juicy as the first, but still a welcome morsel. She caught two beetles and a beetle larva, and she found a big, slimy slug. She did not really enjoy eating slugs, because their slime dirtied her fur and was difficult to clean off, but she was still hungry enough this time. It took her nearly a quarter of an hour to eat the slug and clean up the mess it made.

By now mother mole was quite full. She was not ready to sleep again, but she went back to the nest to find out how the baby moles were getting on. They were still sound asleep, so she set out to hunt again. As she had so recently explored the whole of her system of burrows, she did not find as much food as she had immediately after she first woke up. However, she caught several small insects, and, just before noon, another big worm. She could just manage to eat this, and then she felt quite full once more. She also felt tired and sleepy.

Mother mole went back to the nest. The babies had all woken up, and were crawling clumsily about. Talpa, who was the most restless of them

all, had crawled the furthest, and if his mother
had not come back he might have fallen on to
the cold earth surrounding the nest. She picked
him up with her teeth by the scruff of his neck,
but was very careful not to hurt him or bite
him too hard. All the same, Talpa did not like
being picked up in that way, and he struggled
and gave a little squeak. He was relieved when
she dumped him down in a heap with his brother
and sisters, for he was beginning to feel cold.
Mother mole snuggled down again, and all the
babies had another meal of milk. Then the whole
family, rolled together in a ball, fell asleep
again.

Each day for the mole family was much the
same. The mother mole woke at about eight

o'clock, fed the babies and went out to feed herself until about noon. She then returned to the nest and they all slept for another four hours, until four o'clock in the afternoon. The mother then woke, hunted for food and came back to feed her babies and to sleep at eight in the evening. She slept until midnight, then had four more hours of hunting and feeding, and finally slept from four o'clock until eight o'clock the next morning. And all the time the babies sucked their mother's milk, and slept, and grew bigger and stronger.

2

Talpa Leaves the Nest

On the first of May Talpa was three weeks old. He had grown a lot in the last ten days. He was now four inches long and weighed about a third as much as his mother. So far he had never been outside the nest, and he had fed only on milk. He and his brother and sisters still nestled together most of the time, but they would sometimes crawl around the nest, particularly when they got hungry and their mother was away hunting.

It was eleven o'clock in the morning. It seemed an awfully long time since Talpa had eaten. He and the other young moles – they were too big to be called babies any longer – were all very restless. Talpa decided to go off and try to find his mother. He crawled over the firmly packed hay, which was still warm and soft. Then he came to the end of the nest and fell out suddenly. Although the fall was only about two inches, Talpa was very frightened. He had lived only in a soft warm nest, and now he was sitting on the hard, cold ground. All he wanted was to be back with his brother and sisters.

But then Talpa's brother, who had also tumbled out of the nest, joined him, and the two sisters followed soon after. They were all frightened, and confused. They were neither big enough, nor clever enough, to crawl back, so they tried to keep warm by huddling together under one side of the nest.

Soon mother mole came back from her hunting, to find the nest was empty. She sniffed all round the nest, but she could find none of her children. She scrabbled frantically in the hay, trying to discover if they had burrowed down into it. Then she heard a snuffling noise from outside the nest. It was Talpa, who was hungry and cold and miserable. Quickly mother mole rushed out and pushed her snout under the nest. She was very happy when she found her children, and they were happy to be found. Even though they were quite heavy, she picked them up one at a time with her teeth and dumped them back in the nest. In a few minutes the young moles were warm and comfortable and ready for their milk and sleep.

As their first attempt to crawl out of the nest had been so unpleasant, the young moles did not try again next time they woke up. But by the following day they were even more restless than before, and they were bigger and stronger. So, very carefully, Talpa crawled to the edge of the nest, and instead of falling out carelessly as he had done last time, he scrambled down on to the soil. The others all followed him, and they began to scuffle around in the burrow. After some minutes they felt a little chilly and wished they were back in the nest. This time Talpa, who was always the leader, found he was able with a great effort to climb up and into the nest again. His brother and sisters followed him, so that when mother mole returned, she found all the young moles where she had left them.

By now mother mole was having a difficult time feeding her family. They were so big that they needed more milk than she could make for them, even when she ate every worm and insect she could find. It was time the little moles started to hunt for their own food. So next time she set out to hunt, she took the young ones with her. She did not know that they had already been out in the burrow, but she knew that it was time for them to move. Very gently, she put her nose under Talpa and slowly pushed him to the edge of the nest. Talpa did not know what was happening, nor did he like it very much. But his mother was firm, and out he went, as did the other three.

At first the young moles sat just outside the nest, but then they started to explore the first few inches of the burrow. Their mother had disappeared down the tunnel, but soon they could hear the little noises she made, and sensed with their very sensitive noses that she had returned. And she had brought them a worm to eat.

Up till now Talpa had lived only on milk and no other sort of food. So when his mother tore the worm into little pieces and dropped a small piece in front of him, he did not know what to do. But his mother kept pushing it into his face, and at last he accidentally licked up some of the juice. It tasted delicious. So he quickly gobbled up the bit of the worm, and was glad when his mother gave him another. He wanted more, and got quite angry when there was none, because his mother was teaching the rest of her family to eat worms. Worms are the favourite food of most moles, and it did not take the young moles long to learn to enjoy them.

Now Talpa and the others were able to scamper in and out of the nest whenever they wished. For a day or two they were not very adventurous. They stayed together, and ate only pieces of worm and small insects which their mother found for them. They also slept a good deal in the nest, and drank milk when their mother came home to them. Soon, however, they started to take longer journeys, and found food for themselves as they went along the burrows. Their mother still brought them worms, but they got less and less milk as they began to eat more of other foods.

On the fifteenth of May the young moles had a great adventure. They had been all over the long length of the burrows where their mother hunted, and they could find their way back safely to the nest even from the most distant part, but they had never been outside in the open air. On this day their mother did something new. She dug into the earth at the top of the burrow, in a place where it came very near to the surface of the ground above. She dug the soil with her big, spade-like front paws, shovelling loose earth behind her, which the little moles did not like when it landed on top of them. Soon, however, she got through the roof on to the surface, among a patch of dog's mercury in the middle of the wood.

The little moles quickly followed their mother into the outside world. They could not see the trees and flowers in the way we do, but with their noses they were able to tell a lot about their surroundings. It was a warm sunny day, and they lay and sunbathed for a bit, and then scuffled around among the dead leaves and moss, where they found lots of little worms and insects to eat. After about an hour their mother pushed them one by one back into the burrow, and they scampered back to their nest, very tired but excited.

During the next few days mother mole and young ones had many other outings, in their burrows and sometimes outside. The young were now living entirely on the worms and insects they collected, except once when they had a feast. Their mother had found a dead baby thrush which had fallen out of its nest. She took the young moles along, and they quickly gnawed most of the meat off the bird. This gave them a big meal with less work than was needed when

they had to hunt for worms and beetles.

By May the twentieth, Talpa was quite a big animal. He was half as big and heavy as his mother. His body was covered with thick soft fur that was nearly black, and he looked exactly like a small edition of a grown-up mole.

On May the thirtieth, Talpa's whole life changed. Although at first, when they left the nest, the young animals played together, by now they generally went off separately and preferred to hunt alone. When Talpa met his brother or one of his sisters, they sometimes sniffed each other in a friendly way, but lately they had often taken a quite vicious bite at one another. Even mother mole was less affectionate with her children than she had been, though the whole family still huddled together to sleep in the nest. But today mother mole decided that her offspring must now be independent. She took them out on to the ground in the wood, and gave each one in turn a good nip with her teeth, enough to hurt without doing any real harm to them. They were so surprised that they ran away. Talpa turned back and tried to come down the hole into the burrow to go back to the nest, but his mother was waiting for him. She cuffed him with her paw, and he was afraid she would bite really hard, so he ran away as quickly as he could. Perhaps, too, he was beginning to feel that, as he was nearly grown-up, it was time he went off on his own. So after running for about fifty yards – a long way for a little mole – he dug himself into a dry tussock of grass and fell asleep.

3

Talpa Explores

Talpa slept in his tussock for four hours, then he woke up. Moles usually sleep for four hours, and then hunt for food and move about for the next four, so they really have three "mole days" for every one of our 24-hour days. He was cold and wet with dew, and very hungry. It was midnight by our time, and quite dark, but this did not bother Talpa. He could find his way about just as well in the dark as in bright sunlight.

This was the first time Talpa had ever slept in a tussock all by himself. When he woke up he missed his mother and his brother and sisters, and he missed the warm stuffy nest where he had always slept. But then he remembered that he had to look after himself. So, after a quick

comb of his fur with his paws, and a shake to
to get rid of any grass which was sticking to
him, he set off to explore.

Talpa did not know it, but he was in a small
clearing in the oak wood above his mother's
burrows. There were lots of tunnels hidden
under the wood, and each system of burrows
was inhabited by a grown-up mole. The wood
stretched for some hundreds of acres, and was
surrounded on three sides by flat grass meadows,
with a sluggish river flowing through them.
This was the world which Talpa was to inhabit
for the rest of his life.

Food was the first thing he needed. He sniffed
and scrabbled in the grass where he had slept,
but all he could find was a small green caterpillar, which he ate in one mouthful. It made
him hungrier still. So he moved out into the
open, where the ground was covered with dead
leaves. Under these he found nearly fifty tiny
insects which he snapped up at once, but these
did not satisfy him. In the hollow of a leaf he
found a big drop of water, made by the dew
running together, and he drank this up with
three big gulps. And still he was hungry.

Then, to his delight, he came across a huge
earthworm, lying across the earth, with its tail
anchored in its hole. Talpa was so excited
that he forgot to move quietly and thumped

the ground with his paws as he ran to catch the worm. The worm was frightened by the noise, and in a flash, pulled itself back by its tail and disappeared down its hole. Poor Talpa was disappointed, for he had missed his favourite dinner. And he was still hungry.

After that Talpa moved more carefully. He found a beetle, a millipede and a small slug, which he ate even though it was slimy and rather messy. Then he realized there was another large earthworm just ahead. This time he made no mistake. He crawled up slowly and silently, until he was within an inch of where the worm's tail disappeared into the earth. The rest of the worm was spread out on the ground, and the worm was feeding by rasping the surface from a blade of grass, which it could just reach. Moving faster than he had ever moved before, Talpa sprang. He dug his teeth into the body of the worm, and gripped it with his front paws. The worm tried to escape. It tried to pull its body back into its hole. But Talpa held it too tightly. He pulled the worm away from where it clung to the opening of its hole, so it was helpless and could not resist any more. Talpa gobbled it up head first, just as his mother had done in her burrow.

By now it was four o'clock in the morning. Talpa had enjoyed a good meal, and he felt ready for sleep. At first he longed for his mother's nest and the warmth of his brother and sisters, but he was already beginning to forget them and prefer living alone. He pulled some dead leaves together to give him a bed and some protection, curled up and went to sleep.

The next time he woke up, things did not seem so strange. He smoothed his silky black fur with his paws and set off at once in search of food. He also wanted to find somewhere safer to sleep than a tussock or a heap of oak leaves. It was a warm dry morning, and all the insects were active, so Talpa was quickly able to find something to eat.

He had partly satisfied his appetite when he found a round hole, just big enough for him to crawl into, in a bank covered with yellow primroses. He went down and found himself in a burrow, just like the one where he had lived with his mother. He thought that this would be a fine place to live. Talpa was even more pleased when he caught a big worm lying on the floor of the tunnel. But before he could begin to eat the worm, he had a terrible fright. What seemed to him to be a huge and very fierce mole came rushing down the tunnel, squeaking with rage. Talpa turned tail at once and ran as fast as he could until he had escaped by the same hole as he had come in. He just got out before the angry mole, whose burrow he had invaded, snapped at his tail. Even when he was out of the burrow, he did not stop running until he had found a hiding place under a large stone among the bluebells.

Talpa slept under the stone, and when he woke up he decided to go a long way from the fierce mole's burrow. He walked on through the wood, picking up and eating some wood-lice he found under a small stone, and some ants he caught crossing his path. He soon came to the edge of the wood and out on to a grass field in which some cattle were grazing. Talpa could not actually see the cattle, but he sensed they were there and that they were huge animals from the way the ground shook when they walked. He found that, on this warm day in late spring, there were plenty of fat insect grubs and small worms among the grass, so he had plenty to eat.

But Talpa wanted to get underground, into the sort of burrow he had lived in before. He had tried to get into a burrow another mole had made, and he had been driven out. So he decided that the only thing was to dig a new burrow for himself.

Talpa, like all moles, had big flat paws like spades and strong muscles to dig with. His plan was to make a small hole in the ground, to be

safe and to sleep in when he was not hunting.
He began to dig with both front paws, moving
them together like a person swimming breast
stroke. This pulled him down into the soft earth
just beneath the grass roots. It made him very
tired, and he decided that, for the present, this
little hole would do. He pushed and pulled and
made it a bit bigger, and collected grass to make
a nest. He then crawled into his little nest, and
fell asleep.

4

Danger!

When Talpa woke up, he scuffled round in his little nest, and then came up on to the surface of the field, where he found enough food to satisfy his hunger. He played about by himself in the tussocks for some time, and then went back to his underground nest. Talpa was not at all sleepy yet, so he decided to dig his burrow a bit deeper. He pushed all his bedding out on to the surface, and started to dig. At first he tried to pull himself down into the soil with the sort of breast stroke movement he had used the previous day. But after he had pulled himself halfway into the earth, he found it was too hard, and he could make no more progress. So he then started to dig with one paw at a time. Talpa braced himself against the wall of the burrow

31

with his hind paws, and he pushed his right
front paw firmly down on the earth. Then he
pushed his left paw out in front and pulled it
right back, scooping out a paw full of earth,

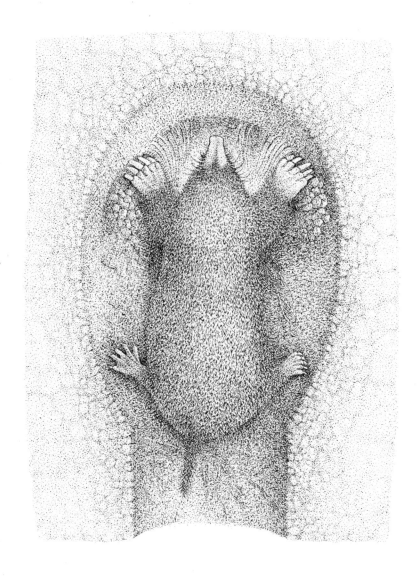

which he pushed behind him. He then dug another scoop of earth with his same paw, and another and another. He had made quite a hole, and had extended the burrow by about a third of his length. His left paw was very tired. But he did not give up. He turned partly on his side, and braced the left paw against the soil. He then started digging, in the same way as before, with his right paw. He dug out four more big scoops of soil, and pushed these behind him. Although he was a bit tired he did not stop. He dug four more times with his left, and then four more times with his right paw. The burrow now extended for about a foot underground.

As he had dug, Talpa had pushed the loose soil behind him, and it now blocked most of the tunnel. He turned round so that he now faced outwards, with the loose soil in front of him. Holding his left paw in front of his face, he pushed the loose soil right out of the little burrow on to the surface. This took several strong pushes with each paw, but at last the tunnel was clear and the soil was outside. Talpa had made his first mole hill. All this work had exhausted him, and he did not even bother to collect any bedding before falling sound asleep on the hard cold earth of the burrow.

Talpa woke up after only about three hours. He was cold, stiff and tired. He had never dug as hard as he had done before he went to sleep, and he had no soft grass to keep him warm. Also he was hungry. He pushed up through the loose earth of the mole hill covering the entrance to his burrow, and went in search of food. It was raining, and soon his fur was wet and bedraggled. He hunted and hunted, with little success. He did find a big black slug, but it was wet with rain and covered in slime, so he left it alone. All he ate were some small beetles, which were rather hard and tough. The rain came down harder and harder, and Talpa decided to go and shelter in his burrow. The rain had made the mole hill muddy, so that it was quite difficult to get down through it, but he did and then lay shivering with cold and wet. He then decided that he must have a proper nest. So he started digging again, not going any deeper this time, but just making a wider room at the end of the burrow. When he went out on to the surface the rain had stopped. He collected a bunch of grass – which was still a bit wet, shook as much water out of it as he could, and took it down below. He did this five times, and in the end he had enough grass to make a really snug nest, even if it was a bit damp. Talpa was tired, and though still hungry, he went to sleep.

He had a good sleep, for about five hours, and when he woke he was warm and felt much better. The warmth of his body had dried the grass. But he now was ravenous. This time he was lucky, for just inside the burrow, underneath the loose soil of the mole hill, he found a big, juicy worm. He seized it at once, and quickly gobbled it up. Then he felt ready to explore. He was still a bit hungry, and he hoped to find some more food. He made a permanent opening in the middle of the mole hill, so he could get in and out quite easily. He then set off into the grass. He did not run out in the open but made a sort of tunnel by pulling himself among the tussocks and roots. He found lots of little worms and insects and soon had eaten all he could manage. Instead of going back to his nest, he curled up among the grass and had a short nap. Then, after sleeping for half an hour, he continued exploring and eating everything he could find, until it was time to make his way back to the nest for a proper long, four-hour sleep.

Talpa lived like this for several days. It was now the middle of June, and the weather was fine and sunny by day, but at night it was cool and the ground was damp with dew. This brought lots of big worms out of their holes, so Talpa had plenty to eat and he grew quickly to his full size. He was over six inches long and weighed nearly a quarter of a pound.

Talpa had not dug any more since he made his nest, in which he slept three times every 24 hours. He spent most of the rest of the time hunting and feeding in the grass. Occasionally he came across a field mouse, but the mice were smaller than Talpa and quickly ran away. Once he met another mole, who was in fact his brother, but the two were not at all pleased to meet one another. Talpa rushed at the other mole and tried to bite his nose, but his brother was too quick and he turned tail and ran away. Talpa felt that he was defending his own patch of ground.

The twentieth of June was nearly Talpa's last day. He had been out feeding, and was just about to go down his burrow to his nest, Suddenly he knew danger was near. We do not know exactly how he became aware of the danger, but he may have detected some vibrations in the air. Whatever the reason, he rushed as fast as he could for his burrow. He was only just in time. A kestrel hawk had spotted him as it hovered overhead, and had dived down from the sky to try to catch him. The hawk's sharp talons tried to seize Talpa, and gave him a nasty scratch on his back, but he was too quick and disappeared underground before the bird could grasp him. The hawk shook itself, and then flew slowly away, up into the sky to look for a bank vole which could not disappear so quickly into the ground.

When Talpa had escaped, he hid deep in his burrow, as far as possible from the fierce kestrel. He had been badly frightened and decided he needed a much longer burrow in which he would be safe from kestrels and owls and other enemies. So after he had had a good sleep, and had regained his strength, he got to work.

5

Talpa Digs his Burrow

Talpa worked very hard for the next ten days, from the twentieth of June until the first of July. As soon as he woke up he went in search of food, first in his burrow and then outside among the grass. The weather was still warm, but there were occasional showers of rain which kept the earth soft and moist, and brought out plenty of worms and insects. As soon as Talpa had found enough food, which might be a big worm in the burrow and a few caterpillars and beetles among the grass, he went down into the earth and started to dig.

His burrow on the twentieth of June was a foot long and ended in the chamber containing the nest. Above ground there was a mole hill marking the entrance. Talpa started digging

39

just to the side of the nest, and he pushed the
loose soil up the burrow so that, when it was
pushed right outside, the mole hill got bigger
and bigger. It took Talpa two days of hard
work, digging all the time he was not sleeping
or hunting for food, to make the tunnel two feet
longer. The longer the tunnel grew, the harder
it was to clear the soil away and push it up into the
mole hill. And the bigger the mole hill, the more
difficult Talpa found it getting in and out. So
he decided to make another hole near the end
of the tunnel, by digging upwards to the surface.
This hole was to be used to get rid of the loose
soil. Digging the shaft was hard work, and, when
he was finished, Talpa scuttled back to his nest
to sleep.

When he woke up Talpa found that all the
loose soil he had dug when he made his vertical
shaft was blocking the tunnel. Although he was

hungry, he started to push the soil upwards and so made his second mole hill. He was lucky and found a worm in the soil, and he snapped it up and went on pushing the earth away. The worm had given him some energy, but he was still hungry when the earth had all been cleared and he went back to the entrance and started hunting among the grass.

Talpa usually fed on worms and insects, even though he liked other things. However, his diet had not had much variety since his mother had found the dead bird many weeks before.

Today, as he was scuffling among the grass, he came upon a big frog resting in the shade of a hogweed leaf. Talpa was quite excited, for a frog would give him several large meals. Frogs, of course, can jump very quickly, and moles do not run very fast, but Talpa decided to try to catch the frog. Also moles do not see as well as do frogs, but their very sensitive noses can detect just where the frog is and where it lands when it jumps.

Talpa ran towards the frog, but the frog jumped away. Talpa ran again, as quickly and quietly as he could, but just as he was going to bite it, the frog jumped again. Talpa would not give up. He ran, and it jumped, and he ran, and it jumped again, until they had gone for nearly twenty yards and had reached the edge of the wood. The frog seemed to be getting tired and at last Talpa caught its hind foot in his mouth. He quickly got hold of its body with his paws, and killed the frog by biting it in the throat. He then made a huge meal by eating all the meat on the left hind leg of the frog.

During the chase Talpa had gone a long way and now he did not know quite where his burrow was. But he set off in the right direction, dragging the remains of the frog with him. He walked for a long time without finding the mole hills or the grass where he usually fed. Finally he recognized a familiar tussock of grass and soon he was at the entrance of the burrow. He pulled the dead frog down into the burrow and left it near the entrance. Then he scuttled along to his nest and fell asleep.

The rest of the dead frog was there ready to be eaten when Talpa woke up. It took him only a few minutes to eat as much as his stomach would hold. Having this large instant food supply gave him more time to dig his burrow. He went along, past the second hole where he had pushed the earth to make the second mole hill, and dug a further two feet. The soil seemed softer and easier to dig, and Talpa was getting stronger. He was able to push all the loose soil back and up to make the second mole hill much bigger before it was time to sleep.

Next time he woke he had another meal of frog, and dug two feet more of the tunnel. He then dug another shaft up to the surface, and pushed the loose earth up to make a third mole hill. The dead frog lasted him for three days and then he pushed its dry bones up into the soil of the first molehill.

So far the burrow had run very nearly straight, keeping about eight inches below the surface. Now Talpa started digging in a sort of zigzag pattern, by starting another branch in a different direction. By the thirtieth of June he had made a complicated tunnel with several branches and with twenty-one mole hills, each about a yard apart. He still used the nest near to the original opening and he usually went out on to the surface by that hole, but as his tunnel got longer he spent more time underground. Now, whenever he awoke from a sleep, he usually found enough worms and insects had collected in the burrow, and he only went out on the surface after exploring all his tunnels to see what was there.

On July the first Talpa decided his burrow was long enough. The meadow where he had burrowed was rich and fertile, and the soil was full of worms. As we have seen, Talpa did not usually dig in search of food, though if he found a worm while digging he ate it. Having dug his tunnel, he simply waited for his food to fall or burrow into it. If he had been living in a field with poor soil, and only a few worms, he would have had to make a much longer burrow, in order to get enough to eat.

The cows in the field did not bother about Talpa. They did not like his mole hills, because they covered some of the grass with soil and made it nasty to eat, but there was plenty of other grass. Once where Talpa had made his burrow nearer to the surface than usual, only about three inches down, a cow's hoof broke through the roof. But Talpa had plenty of time to escape, and when the cow went away he dug a new bit of burrow deeper down so as to avoid the danger.

Talpa now had quite a lazy time. There was plenty of food, and he only had to run along the burrow to find it. He did no more hard

digging. When he had eaten enough he dozed
for a bit, then walked along and ate another
worm, and then he had another sleep. Talpa's
fur grew sleek and silky, and he became a little
fatter and heavier.

6

A Trap

The twenty-one mole hills made quite a mess
of the grass in the field and left less for the cows
to eat. The farmer who owned the cows did not
like moles, and decided to get rid of Talpa. On
the morning of July the third he went into his
barn and found a mole trap hanging on a rusty
nail on the wall. The trap was a cruel one, made
of grey galvanized iron. It had two jaws and a
strong spring. There was a metal plate, which
held the jaws apart, but when this was touched
it fell out and – snap – the jaws caught any
animal that was within their grasp.

The farmer went along to the field, carrying
his trap, his walking stick and a trowel. He went
to the middle part of the field where the mole
hills appeared, and tried to find the burrow

Talpa had dug beneath the ground. He knew that the burrow, which he called a mole run, ran from one mole hill to the next. Trying to find it, he pushed his stick down into the earth between two mole hills. At first it went right down into solid earth, but next time he found the burrow, When the stick had gone down about eight inches he could tell it was the burrow because the stick went in for the next four inches without needing to be pushed. The farmer pulled out his stick, and then, with his trowel, made a hole about six inches wide, right down into the soil so that he could see the mole run. He knew that Talpa was using this burrow, because the earth was soft and covered with the pattern of a mole's feet.

The farmer started to set the trap. He took great care to remove any loose lumps of earth that had fallen into the burrow. Then he set the trap, carefully arranging the metal plate – which was a sort of trigger – so that the slightest touch would set it off and kill a mole between the jaws. Then, very slowly, he put the trap down into the mole run. The first time he tried to do this he was a bit clumsy, and he set off the trap himself. But next time he was more careful, and he put the trap, properly set, down into Talpa's run. He knew that a mole is not easy to catch, and often finds traps if the hole above them is

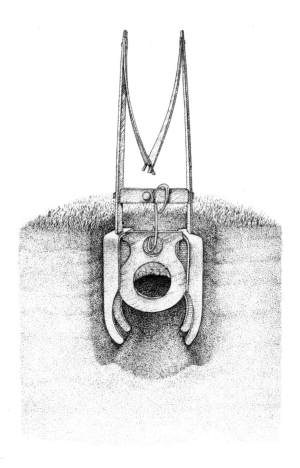

not carefully filled in. So he got some small lumps of turf and filled the hole carefully, taking care that no light and no draughts of air could get down it. The two arms of the trap stuck about six inches above the ground. These arms make it easy to tell if the trap is still set, or if it has sprung and may have caught a mole, because they then open out wide as the jaws close together to catch the animal. The farmer thought he had set the trap very cleverly, so he collected the cows and drove them home to be milked.

Soon after the trap had been set, Talpa woke up and started to run along his burrow looking for food. He found three large "leather-jackets" – or grubs which, if they are not eaten by moles, will turn into daddy-long-legs flies. Then he came on the trap, and nearly ran smack into the trigger plate. That would have been the end of Talpa. But fortunately he was very alert; if he had been just going back to sleep after having run about for four hours he would probably have been caught. He stopped still in his tracks about two inches from the trap. Then he moved forward very slowly and sniffed at the un-familiar object, which he knew had not been there last time he had run that way. Talpa did not know it was a trap, but he knew that un-familiar things may be dangerous. And the trap had a curious, rather unpleasant smell from the tobacco that the farmer had been smoking.

Talpa decided not to go any nearer. He started digging into the side of the burrow, and produced a lot of loose soil. He did not push this earth up into one of his mole hills, but he shoved it gently into the trap, so that it blocked up the jaws. It also blocked up the tunnel. Talpa knew that his burrow ran on beyond the trap, so he dug a new loop, which avoided the trap, and soon broke out into the old tunnel beyond it. He cleared up all the soil he had dug by pushing it into the trap, making it quite useless. And for the rest of that day Talpa moved up and down his burrows very carefully, in case there were any more hidden dangers.

The next morning, when the farmer came to collect his cows to be milked, he went to see whether he had caught a mole in his trap. The two arms stuck up straight, so he knew that he had not been successful. But he did not know that Talpa had filled the trap with earth. Because he thought it was still set properly, he left it in the burrow, hoping that it would catch a mole the next day.

After several days the farmer began to get suspicious. He thought that the mole might have gone away, or have been caught by an owl if it had come out of its burrow at night. So he opened up the hole to check on his trap. When he found that Talpa had bunged the trap full of soil, he was furious. He threw the trap on the ground, and instead of setting it again, he left it in the grass, where it was eventually trodden into the earth by one of the cows, and so lost.

When Talpa came back to the place where he had filled the trap with earth, he found a big hole open to the surface. He sniffed around cautiously until he was sure there was no danger,

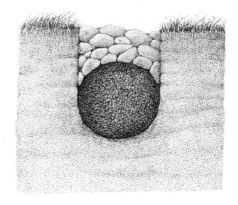

then he carefully repaired the damage by taking
pieces of sticky soil as big as walnuts and build-
ing them up to roof over the broken burrow.

  The farmer was still angry, but he did not
bother to look for his trap. And as he did not
see any new mole hills, he thought that the mole
had gone. But Talpa had a long run underground, and he could find quite enough food
without digging any more. In fact he was finding far more worms than he could eat, so he
decided to store them in order to have food
when hunting was bad. He dug a little room,
much smaller than his nest, only about two
inches across, in the side of his tunnel. Every
time he found a large worm which he did not
want to eat, he bit off its head and pushed it into
the storeroom. The worms could not escape
by burrowing when their heads had been bitten,

but they did not die, and in a few days started to grow new heads. Soon Talpa had nearly fifty worms in his storeroom. He was very content, well fed and comfortable.

7

The Flood

The fine, warm weather continued until July the eighth. Then it started to rain, and it rained without stopping for two days. At first this did not worry Talpa. A few drops trickled down into his burrow, and in places the floor became quite muddy. But the mole has fur which does not easily pick up mud, and Talpa managed to keep himself clean and sleek. There was plenty to eat, and he added a few headless worms to his store.

Talpa did not know, but the rain was falling heavily all over the country, particularly in the hills. The water ran off the fields into the streams, and these became raging torrents, which were then running into the river that had been meandering peacefully along at the bottom of the field where Talpa had his burrow. The river was rising, and the water was flowing rapidly. It had already washed away a lot of water plants that grew along the banks, and even some of the willow trees, growing with their pink roots in the water, had been uprooted and were riding on the waves and going down to the sea. The moorhens had all retreated to the small ponds in the fields, and even the heron could catch no fish in the brown, turbulent and muddy water.

By the morning of July the tenth the river had overflowed its banks. The rain had actually stopped falling, but the river continued to rise for several days as the water seeped out of the ground and ran off the surface of the uplands. The field started to flood. The farmer realized what was happening, and drove his cows away to another field on higher ground on the side of the hill. He knew what floods meant in the fenland. Talpa did not, but he was soon to find out.

The water rose and rose, flooding more and more of the field. At three o'clock in the afternoon the first wave reached Talpa's first mole hill and washed it away. This did not matter,

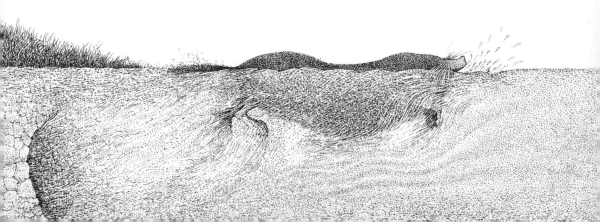

and Talpa did not know what had happened. But a few minutes later water started to run down into the burrow. It started as a slow trickle, and filled up only the lowest parts of the tunnels, though Talpa's nest was soaked. Talpa was sound asleep, and he had a very uncomfortable awakening. He jumped up and ran until he found a dry stretch of burrow. He sat there for a moment, and then the water came rushing towards him. Talpa ran in panic along the tunnel, half wading and half swimming. He came to a shaft leading up to a mole hill and to the surface. Trying to escape, he scrambled up and pushed the loose, wet earth aside. This was the worst thing he could have done, for it let the flood water rush in from above. Talpa was washed down the shaft and into the burrow. The water continued to pour in, and Talpa was completely submerged. He could not breathe, and he choked and nearly drowned.

When the tunnel was full, the water became quite still, and Talpa was not buffetted about any more, although he was still frightened and faint from lack of air. He decided to make one last desperate effort to escape. He pushed against the wall and found himself back at the bottom of the shaft. Then just when he was nearly ready to give up and drown, he found the hole, and this time climbed up without too much difficulty. At the top he popped out of the hole and bobbed up on the surface of the flood.

Moles are very good swimmers because of their big flat front paws. Talpa set off vigorously swimming breast strokes away from his flooded burrow. We do not know how he knew in which direction to swim, but he went towards the high ground at the south end of the field. He had nearly half a mile to go, and he swam on and on for nearly half an hour. Although exhausted, he had to reach dry land.

At last Talpa's feet touched the top of the submerged grass, and then the firm ground. He was soaked, tired and famished, but he knew he must first find safety. He was unaware that a huge heron was near, and had already caught another mole as it landed on the bank some fifty yards away. Herons are very fond of eating moles when they can catch them, though moles are safe when underground in their burrows.

Talpa ran quickly up the bank. He found a soft place in the soil under a hawthorn bush and burrowed into the ground as quickly as he could. He scooped up the soil with all his might, and sent it flying behind him, like a small volcano, until he was nearly a foot underground. Then, exhausted, he fell asleep.

Poor Talpa was miserable when he woke up. He had lost his snug burrow with his warm nest

and his food store. (The worms he had left behind
in his burrow were not all drowned. In a few
weeks they grew new heads and escaped by
burrowing into the ground.) Talpa crept out
of the ground very slowly and carefully, because
he did not know what enemies might be about.
His first need was for food. In his search, he was
lucky, because he found a dead field mouse
which had been drowned in the flood and then
washed ashore. Talpa dragged the dead mouse

59

into the little burrow he had made the night before, and had a good meal of its flesh. He did not feel like starting to dig a proper burrow yet, but he did make a new underground nest, in which he could sleep safely. Then he went to explore. He soon found himself at the edge of the flood, near to the point where he had landed a few hours before. But he felt that he had had enough swimming, so he went to his new home and slept.

For the next week, until the seventeenth of July, Talpa lived in the same place. The rain had stopped entirely, and the weather became very hot. Each day he went down to the edge of the flood, and each day he had to go a bit further to find the water. The river was beginning to fall. The grass was very wet, and the soil was muddy, but plenty of big worms had drowned and their bodies lay on the surface. A great many rooks and other birds flew down to share the feast, but there were still plenty for Talpa to eat, and he began to think things were not so bad after all. But he also felt it was time he had a new, permanent, safe home, a home in which he would not be drowned if there was another flood.

8

Home

The seventeenth of July was a hot, dry day. Talpa woke up, came out of his nest and started to hunt for food. The grass was too dry for there to be any worms or slugs in it, but there were plenty of beetles and ants running busily about, and Talpa soon found enough food to satisfy him. Then he set off to find a home. He did not go back to his burrow in the meadow, and even if he had, he would have found it was full of water and mud. He went along the hedgerow in which his nest had been hidden. Talpa knew he would be safe from hawks and herons if he kept under the shade of the hedgerow bushes. The ground was rough and there were a lot of big stones, but he trudged on for nearly an hour. He could only go slowly because he had to climb over bits of broken wood, and he tried to avoid the puddles still filled with dirty water. Once he came to a gate, where the ground was bare, offering no protective covering. The farmer drove his cows through this gate, and their hooves had worn away the grass and trampled up the mud. Talpa was frightened at being out in the open but he ran quickly across the bare ground and went back into the rough grass in the hedge on the other side of the gate.

He rested for a quarter of an hour, and was glad to find a big caterpillar to eat. Fortunately the ground was not so rough now, and after walking another twenty minutes he reached the oak wood in which he had been born. He decided to try to find a burrow in the earth. When he had left the wood in May, the bluebells had still been in flower, and the oak trees had only a thin covering of light green leaves. Now it was summer. The trees cast a dense shade, and the plants were full grown. There were nettles, on which he stung his tender nose, and ferns, and, in the little clearings where the sun could reach, big tussocks of dense grass.

Last time Talpa had been in the wood, he had found a burrow but had been driven out of it by a large, fierce mole. So now when he found a hole leading underground, he sniffed cautiously and waited to see if there was any danger.

After a few minutes, when nothing had happened, he started to crawl down, very slowly and carefully, into the hole. Talpa was now much bigger and stronger than he had been in May, and if he had found another mole in the burrow he might have had a fight and tried to drive it away. But this time he was lucky. The mole who had lived in this burrow had gone out looking for worms during the previous night, and had been caught by a big tawny owl. The mole had been eaten by the two young owls, now able to fly but still living with their mother in a nest built in a hole in an old oak tree.

Talpa soon knew that he had found just what he wanted. The burrow ran for ten yards in an almost straight line from the hole by which he entered, and then it branched to the left and to the right. Along the left branch he found a nest full of dried oak leaves. Although Talpa was getting sleepy, he went on exploring until he had covered the whole length of all the burrows in his new territory. He learned all its twists and turns, and was soon able to run quickly without ever bumping into a wall or missing a bend. He found several worms on the floor, and he ate one or two, but then he went into the nest and fell asleep at once.

The burrow Talpa had found had been dug originally by a large male mole nearly a hundred years before. This mole had lived in it for five years, and then he had died. Since then, some forty different moles had lived, one at a time, for several years, in the same burrow. The moles had not had to dig very much. They had repaired the tunnels when the soil fell in, and they had sometimes dug an extension if food seemed to be scarce. Talpa had found a very comfortable, well established old burrow for his home.

There was very little sign of Talpa's burrow to be seen on the ground in the wood. At one point the tunnel passed under a grassy path, and here the earth was cracked and, if you looked very carefully, you could see where the last mole had mended the roof. In one or two places there were the remains of old mole hills, but they had nearly washed away in the rain. These mole hills had been made of the soil dug up when a piece of the burrow had to be repaired. Most people walking through the wood would have no idea that Talpa was scampering about, feeding on worms, and sleeping every four hours, in his dark, warm burrow nearly a foot beneath the surface.

It was July when Talpa found his home. The days and the weeks went by. September and October were warm and dry, and he had an easy, uneventful life. Four hours to sleep, four hours to wake and feed, then four hours more sleep.

He hardly ever came up out of his burrow, for he found plenty to eat by just walking up and down the burrow and picking up worms and beetles. It rained a lot in November, but very little water seeped into the burrow.

At the beginning of December the weather turned very cold. For several days Talpa did not notice it, but then it became cold in his burrow as well. The cold weather made the worms and insects sluggish, and they burrowed down deeper into the earth, where it was warmer. As they were not near the surface, very few fell into Talpa's burrow. For two days Talpa found little to eat, and he was hungry. Then he found a hole in the floor of the burrow, and when he pushed his way in he found that it led to a deep tunnel, two feet below the surface of the ground. This was an old burrow which had been dug many years before. It had not been used by a mole for a long time, and loose soil from the roof and walls had fallen and was partly block-ing it in some places. Talpa quickly cleared the soil away, pushing it in front of him into the upper tunnel in which he had been living, and then up a shaft to make a new mole hill on the ground in the wood. Moles living in permanent burrows sometimes make new mole hills when they are cleaning out disused tunnels in cold weather. People sometimes think that they have been digging in the hard, frozen soil, but of course they have been working deep down in the warm earth.

Some of the worms that had dug down deeply now dropped into Talpa's new burrows and satisfied his hunger. He made a new nest in the lower burrow, and the only time he went outside in December was to collect dry leaves for his bedding. At the beginning of January there was a deep fall of snow. This covered the ground in the wood, and all over the countryside, with a thick white blanket. It soon became much warmer under the snow, so Talpa could feed in his upper tunnels again. One day he decided to come out on the surface, and he found the opening to the tunnel covered with snow. Talpa had no idea what the snow was, but it was soft and he could burrow through it at a terrific speed. He enjoyed playing in the snow, and making long burrows in it, for several days. Then the thaw came, the snow melted, and Talpa stayed safe and warm in his home.

9

Talpa Seeks a Mate

January and February were cold, and there were more snow falls. Talpa stayed in his burrow, eating and sleeping day after day. Then it was March. The days got longer, though Talpa did not see the lengthening daylight. The dog's mercury plants in the wood sent up bright green spikes, and in sheltered places primrose flowers were to be seen. Spring was coming soon.

Talpa began to feel restless. He had his comfortable burrow, and plenty of food. His nests – for he had one in the upper tunnel, and the new one he had made last December in the lower – were warm and snug. But he began to feel that he wanted to come out and move about in the world. He did not understand at first that what he really wanted was to find a female mole for his mate.

On the fifth of March Talpa came up on the surface above his burrow, and started exploring the wood. The first day he spent three hours outside, and then he went down his hole again and slept in his nest. Next time he woke, after a good meal of worms found in the burrow, he climbed out again, and this time he went much further. When it was time to sleep, he was a long way from home. Fortunately the weather was warm, so he made a rough nest with leaves among the roots of an oak tree and went to sleep.

When he woke, it was the seventh of March. By this time Talpa knew that he was hunting for a female mole. Ever since he had left his mother, nearly a year ago, he had been quite alone, and had quarrelled or even fought with every mole he had met. He had disliked all moles, both other males and females. But it was now the breeding season, when male and female moles meet without fighting each other.

For some days, Talpa could not find a mate. He crawled down into every burrow he could find, but every time he was driven out by another male mole. Moles are very fierce when they defend their own territory, and Talpa, who knew he was trespassing, did not really wish to fight. If another male mole had tried to come into his home, he would have attacked it with all his might and driven it away.

By March the tenth, Talpa was getting im-
patient. Although it was warm weather for
March, it was cold at night, especially when
living above the ground without a proper nest.
It was difficult to find enough food. The worms
stayed underground, and there were not many
insects. Fortunately he found a dead squab – a
baby wood pigeon – which had fallen from its
nest and died, and this gave him several good
meals. Otherwise he was often cold and hungry.

Then he found another opening into a
burrow, and he crawled in, though he did not
know what he was going to find. He walked
softly and gently along the burrow, sniffing as
he went, for he would be able to detect a female
mole by her smell. He thought there might be
a female mole about two yards away down the
tunnel, but he was not sure. He stopped and
sniffed again. Then he was sure. The female
mole, who had been hoping that a male mole
would come down the burrow, had smelt him
at the same time. The two animals ran towards
each other and hugged each other with their
paws. They did not bite each other, but played
gently for some time. Then the female led Talpa
along to her nest, which was very soft and
warmly lined with moss.

The two moles mated and stayed together
the next few hours. In about three weeks the

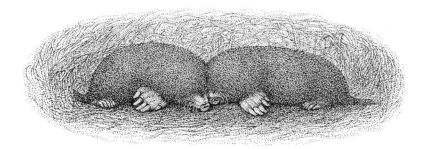

female would give birth to four new baby moles.

The moles slept, and went out in the burrow together and found worms to eat, and then went back to sleep together in the nest. When they woke up the second time, they were ready to separate. The female mole was not vicious, but she started pushing Talpa out of her nest, and even gave him a small, sharp bite. Talpa also knew that it was time to go, and to resume his solitary life. So he scuttled off down the tunnel and out into the wood.

The female mole remained in her burrow, and in April her babies were born and lived with her just as Talpa and his brother and sisters had lived with their mother a year before. Talpa never saw his offspring. Male moles never help to bring up their young, and if a male mole ever finds a baby mole he will probably kill and eat it.

Talpa soon found his way back to his home burrow. But when he got there, he discovered that another male mole had moved in and was sleeping in his nest. Talpa was very angry. He attacked the intruder, who was still asleep, and gave him a fierce bite in the back of the neck. The other mole tried to turn around and bite Talpa, but he was not quick enough. Talpa gave him another bite, and hit him as hard as he could, first with his left, and then with his right paw. The intruder had had enough, and he ran away as fast as he could. Talpa had recaptured his territory. He explored all the burrows to make sure they were in good order, he ate all the worms he could find, and then he crawled into his nest. He scuffled round and round in the leaves to make himself comfortable, and then he went to sleep, happy to be home again.

10

A Mole Alone

It was the tenth of April again, and Talpa was now one year old. It had been an eventful year. He had been born, and had lived together with his mother and his brother and two sisters for a few weeks, and then he had set off, alone, to find a home. He had dug a long burrow, and made a nest. When the floods had come, he had lost his first home and had then made a new burrow, and a new nest. He had gone in search of a mate, and now he was the father of a family of little moles, which he would never see. Now he was back in his own burrow, with plenty of space, two comfortable nests, and lots of worms to eat. Would he be lonely? Would he miss his mate, his family, all the other moles?

No. This is how moles live. They usually like

to be by themselves. This is why they bite and drive away any mole which tries to come into their own burrow. Moles live happily together for a few weeks when they are babies, and the adults meet to mate once a year, and that is all they need. Moles are very independent and solitary animals.

We do not know exactly what will happen to Talpa. He is a healthy, strong mole, and he will probably live for another five years. He will probably stay in his burrow from April of each year until the following March, when he will go out in search of a mate. After mating, he will come back to his own burrow. At the age of four or five years, moles are quite old, and they are not as quick and agile as they were before. Wild animals do not often live into old age, when they find it difficult to survive.

Talpa will probably be killed by a tawny owl, and then eaten by her babies. In the wild, animals have to eat to survive. Talpa will have eaten hundreds of worms and thousands of insects during his lifetime, and it is only natural that before he gets old and feeble, he too will be eaten by the young owls who also live in the wood on the edge of the fen.